I0781411

Alexander Hamilton:
Forging the Foundations of a Nation

Alexander Hamilton, one of the most influential figures in American history, was born on January 11, 1757, in the British West Indies on the island of Nevis. Although he is widely celebrated as a Founding Father of the United States, his origins were far from the American mainland.

Hamilton's childhood was marked by adversity and hardship. His parents were not married, and his father, James Hamilton, abandoned the family when Alexander was just a child. His mother, Rachel Faucette Lavien, struggled to provide for her two sons, Alexander and James Jr. Tragedy struck the family when Rachel passed away from a fever, leaving the young Alexander an orphan at the age of 11.

To overcome these early challenges, Hamilton displayed remarkable initiative and secured a position as a clerk at a trading company, where his sense of responsibility quickly became evident. While working in this role, he wrote a remarkable letter to his estranged father about a devastating hurricane in Christiansted. This letter was so compelling that it was published in the Royal Danish-American Gazette. Its eloquence and depth of thought impressed local leaders, who recognized Hamilton's exceptional writing talent and decided to support his further education.

In 1772, at the age of 15, Hamilton arrived in New York City, a bustling colonial hub. Here, the

ambitious and self-reliant youth began to lay
the foundation for his remarkable future. He
attended Elizabethtown Academy in New Jersey,
where he swiftly gained a reputation
as a gifted student.

During the early 1770s, as tensions between
the American colonies and Britain reached a
critical point, Hamilton immersed himself in the
political and intellectual currents of the time.
His involvement with a local militia and his
remarkable writing abilities soon earned him
recognition. In 1774, at the age of 17,
he published his first political pamphlet,
"A Full Vindication of the Measures of Congress,"
passionately supporting the revolutionary cause
for American independence from British
colonial rule.

By 1776, as the American Revolution gained
momentum, Hamilton joined the Continental Army.
His leadership and organizational skills were
immediately evident, and he quickly rose
through the ranks to become an aide-de-camp to
General George Washington, the Commander-in-
Chief. This position allowed him to observe
firsthand the challenges facing the fledgling
nation.

Hamilton's contributions extended beyond
the battlefield. He became a prolific writer,
crafting influential essays and letters
advocating for a stronger federal government.
His vision for a more centralized and
financially stable country would later become
one of the cornerstones of American governance.

In 1780, Hamilton married Elizabeth Schuyler, the daughter of a prominent New York family. Elizabeth not only supported his political ideals but also played a crucial role in assisting with his later publishing efforts. Additionally, their marriage significantly bolstered Hamilton's social and political connections. Over the years, they had eight children together, further cementing their family life.

The Architect of American Finance

Hamilton's post-war career began with his appointment as the first Secretary of the Treasury in 1789 under President George Washington. In this role, he faced immense challenges. The young nation was burdened with war debts and financial instability, threatening its survival. Hamilton proposed a series of bold and controversial measures, collectively known as the Hamiltonian economic program.

One of his most significant achievements was the establishment of a national bank, the First Bank of the United States. This institution laid the foundation for a stable national currency, centralized financial control, and facilitated economic growth. Although his financial plans faced fierce opposition, they were ultimately adopted and set the United States on a path to economic prosperity.

Hamilton's contributions extended to his role as a key author of the Federalist Papers. In partnership with James Madison and John Jay, he penned a series of essays advocating for the

ratification of the U.S. Constitution.
These essays articulated the principles of
federalism and the necessity of a strong central
government. Hamilton's writings, particularly
in The Federalist No. 1, remain relevant and
instructive in understanding the
Constitution's intent.

His Federalist beliefs clashed with the views
of his political rival, Thomas Jefferson.
Hamilton, as a Federalist, believed in a strong
federal government, a national bank, and a broad
interpretation of the Constitution, while
Jefferson, an Anti-Federalist, championed a
strict interpretation of the Constitution,
agrarian society, and states' rights. This
rivalry culminated in a fiercely partisan
political climate and the formation of the
first political parties in the United States.

Hamilton's tenure as Secretary of the Treasury
ended in 1795, but his influence did not wane.
He continued to advocate for strong federal
governance and contributed to the development
of the nation's financial infrastructure,
including the founding of the U.S. Mint.
Additionally, he was instrumental in the
establishment of maritime security (precursor
to the U.S. Coast Guard) saying "A few armed
vessels...might at a small expense be made useful
sentinels of the laws."

Tragically, Hamilton's life was cut short in a
notorious duel with Vice President Aaron Burr
on July 11, 1804, in Weehawken, New Jersey.
The duel, which was the tragic culmination of
their longstanding political and personal

animosities, resulted in Hamilton's death.
He succumbed to his injuries a day later on
July 12, at the age of 47, marking the end
of a remarkable and impactful life.

Alexander Hamilton's impact on the United States
remains profound. His vision of a strong federal
government, a national banking system, and a
thriving industrial economy continues to shape
the nation's policies and institutions.
The enduring influence of his ideas and
contributions, both to the American financial
system and the nation's constitutional
foundations, is a testament to his lasting
mark on the course of American history.

Major Ideas and Philosophy
of Alexander Hamilton

STRONG FEDERAL GOVERNMENT: Alexander
Hamilton's unwavering support for a robust
federal government, rather than ceding power
to the states, stemmed from his belief that it was
the linchpin of national stability and progress.
In his view, a strong central authority was
essential for maintaining order, upholding the
rule of law, and fostering economic development.
He saw it as the means to unify the young nation
and provide the necessary framework for its
growth. His convictions on this matter were
evident in his instrumental role in drafting the
U.S. Constitution and in his contributions to
The Federalist Papers, where he made a
compelling case for the ratification of the
Constitution by emphasizing the advantages
of a powerful federal government.

NATIONAL BANK: Hamilton's proposal for a
national bank was not merely a financial
institution; it was a cornerstone of his economic
vision for the United States. He believed that
a national bank would offer stability to the
fledgling financial system, serving as a
dependable repository for the government's
funds. Moreover, it would provide a conduit for
government borrowing, allowing it to finance
projects and stimulate economic growth.
Hamilton's vision was more than monetary;
it was a strategic move to secure the nation's
fiscal health, setting the stage for a robust
and dynamic economy.

ECONOMIC DIVERSIFICATION AND
INDUSTRIALIZATION: Hamilton's advocacy for
economic diversification and industrialization
reflected his ambition to transform the United
States into a formidable economic force.
He recognized the importance of a diversified
economy and a thriving manufacturing sector
in reducing the nation's dependence on foreign
goods. In his view, industrialization was the
engine that would drive economic growth, create
jobs, and provide the country with the means to
compete on the global stage. To achieve this,
Hamilton proposed using protective tariffs
and government subsidies as tools to encourage
domestic industry, paving the way for a more
self-reliant and prosperous nation. For
instance, the Tariff of 1816, the first protective
tariff in U.S. history, served the purpose of
nurturing domestic manufacturing by shielding
it from foreign competition, particularly
in the aftermath of the War of 1812, laying
the groundwork for future industrial growth.

PUBLIC DEBT: Alexander Hamilton's approach to public debt was driven by his goal of establishing the creditworthiness of the young United States. He believed that by assuming and paying off the states' Revolutionary War debts, often accomplished through methods like land sales and taxes on luxury items, especially whiskey, the nation could foster trust among creditors and attract crucial investment. Hamilton's vision was to make the United States an enticing destination for capital and to instill confidence in its financial stability. This strategic approach was more than a fiscal maneuver; it was a pivotal step in securing the nation's financial future. Additionally, the Compromise of 1790 played a crucial role in this financial strategy, as it resulted in the relocation of the U.S. capital to Washington, D.C., in exchange for southern support for assuming state debts, further strengthening the federal government's financial footing.

IMPLIED POWERS AND LOOSE CONSTRUCTION OF THE CONSTITUTION: Hamilton's views on constitutional interpretation were a reflection of his pragmatic approach to governance. He favored a broad interpretation of the Constitution, emphasizing the "necessary and proper" clause as a means to empower the federal government with flexible authority. He believed that the Constitution should not be interpreted too rigidly and that the federal government possessed powers beyond those explicitly delineated. This perspective allowed for a more adaptable and versatile approach to governance, enabling the government to address the ever-evolving challenges of a growing and complex nation.

MERITOCRACY VS ELITISM: Alexander Hamilton's philosophy leaned more towards elitism than meritocracy. He believed that individuals with education and wealth were better suited to guide the nation, as they were more likely to act in the best interests of the country. While Hamilton recognized the importance of talent and ability, he placed a strong emphasis on the role of the educated and affluent elite in leadership and decision-making. He saw this as a means of promoting stability and progress, with the belief that these individuals were better equipped to make choices that would benefit the broader population and advance the nation's interests. Hamilton's view underscored the importance of a select class of leaders in shaping the course of the young United States.

STRONG MILITARY AND NAVAL FORCE: Hamilton recognized the importance of a strong and well-organized military in safeguarding the nation's interests and maintaining its security. He believed that a disciplined and capable military was crucial not only for self-defense but also for projecting strength globally. This conviction led him to play a pivotal role in the early organization of the U.S. military as well as maritime security, advocating for professional training, discipline, and a standing army to ensure the country's readiness and protection.

FOREIGN POLICY: Hamilton's foreign policy doctrine was characterized by a preference for strengthening ties with Great Britain. He believed that a close relationship with Britain would bring economic advantages and enhance American security. His rationale was based on Britain's status as a major global power at the time. However, this approach was contentious due to the ongoing tensions between Britain and France, which culminated in the Napoleonic Wars. The disagreement over foreign policy contributed to the development of political parties in the United States, with Hamilton's Federalists supporting closer ties with Britain and Thomas Jefferson's Democratic-Republicans favoring a more pro-French stance.

AGRARIAN SOCIETY VS. URBANIZATION: Hamilton's vision for the United States leaned heavily towards urbanization and industrialization. He saw cities and industries as the engines of economic growth and believed that these developments were essential for the nation's self-sufficiency and prosperity. In contrast, his political rival, Thomas Jefferson, championed the idea of an agrarian society, valuing rural agriculture and self-sufficiency as the foundation of American life. This ideological difference contributed to the early political divisions in the United States, with Hamilton's urban and industrial orientation prevailing in the long run and marking the nation's transition from an agrarian economy to an industrial powerhouse.

JUDICIAL SYSTEM: Hamilton played a significant role in shaping the federal judiciary. His work on The Federalist Papers, particularly Federalist No. 78, laid out arguments for the independence and importance of the judiciary in interpreting the Constitution. His vision laid the groundwork for the federal judiciary's essential role in interpreting the Constitution and providing legislative checks, reinforcing the balance of powers within the American government.

Alexander Hamilton's ideas and philosophy, grounded in a belief in a strong federal government, a robust economy, and a dynamic society, had a profound and lasting impact on the development of the United States, and many of his principles continue to shape the nation's policies and institutions to this day.

This book of quotes is a testament to the enduring wisdom and insight of Alexander Hamilton. They offer a window into the mind of a man who helped lay the foundation of a great nation and whose influence still resonates through the corridors of history. Join us on a journey through the profound words of a remarkable statesman as we explore the essence of Alexander Hamilton through his own quotes.

The sacred rights of
mankind are not to be
rummaged for among old
parchments or musty
records. They are
written, as with a
sunbeam, in the whole
volume of human
nature, by the hand of
the divinity itself;
and can never be
erased.

Constitutions should consist only of general provisions; the reason is that they must necessarily be permanent, and that they cannot calculate for the possible change of things.

Men often oppose a
thing merely because
they have had no agency
in planning it, or
because it may have
been planned by those
whom they dislike.

Great Ambition,
unchecked by
principle, or the
love of Glory, is an
unruly Tyrant...

Opinion,
whether well
or ill-founded,
is the governing
principle of
human affairs.

As riches increase and
accumulate in few hands, as
luxury prevails in society,
virtue will be in a greater
degree considered as only a
graceful appendage of wealth,
and the tendency of things
will be to depart from the
republican standard. This is
the real disposition of human
nature; it is what neither the
honorable member nor myself
can correct. It is a common
misfortune that awaits our
State constitution,
as well as all others.

Experience is the
oracle of truth; and
where its responses
are unequivocal, they
ought to be conclusive
and sacred.

The President of the United States would be liable to be impeached, tried, and upon conviction of treason, bribery, or other high crimes and misdemeanors, removed from office; and would afterwards be liable to prosecution and punishment in the ordinary course of law. The person of the King of Great Britain is sacred and inviolable: There is no constitutional tribunal to which he is amenable, no punishment to which he can be subjected without involving the crisis of a national revolution.

If you understood
the natural rights of
mankind, you would be
convinced that natural
liberty is a gift of the
beneficent Creator to the
whole human race, and that
civil liberty is founded
in that, and cannot be
wrested from any people
without the most manifest
violation of justice.

The loss of liberty
to a generous mind
is worse than death.

In the general
course of human
nature, a power over
a man's subsistence
amounts to a power
over his will.

The desire of reward is one of the strongest incentives of human conduct;... the best security for the fidelity of mankind is to make their interest coincide with their duty.

We must make the best
of those ills which
cannot be avoided.

I have thought it my
duty to exhibit
things as they are,
not as they ought to
be.

The creation of crimes
after the commission of
the fact, or, in other
words, the subjecting of
men to punishment for
things which, when they
were done, were breaches
of no law, and the
practice of arbitrary
imprisonments, have been,
in all ages, the favorite
and most formidable
instruments of tyranny.

This balance between
the National and State
governments ought to be
dwelt on with peculiar
attention, as it is of the
utmost importance. It forms
a double security to the
people. If one encroaches
on their rights they will
find a powerful protection
in the other. Indeed, they
will both be prevented
from overpassing their
constitutional limits by a
certain rivalship, which
will ever subsist
between them.

All political power is inherent in the people. Government is instituted for the protection, security, and benefit of the people, and they have the right at all times to alter or reform the same, whenever the public good may require it.

Government is
frequently and
aptly classed under
two descriptions-a
government of force,
and a government of
laws; the first is
the definition of
despotism-the last,
of liberty.

Why has government
been instituted at all?
Because the passions of
man will not conform
to the dictates of
reason and justice
without constraint.

Wise politicians will be
cautious about fettering
the government with
restrictions that cannot
be observed, because they
know that every break of
the fundamental laws,
though dictated by
necessity, impairs that
sacred reverence which
ought to be maintained
in the breast of rulers
towards the constitution
of a country.

Good constitutions are formed upon a comparison of the liberty of the individual with the strength of government: If the tone of either be too high, the other will be weakened too much. It is the happiest possible mode of conciliating these objects, to institute one branch peculiarly endowed with sensibility, another with knowledge and firmness. Through the opposition and mutual control of these bodies, the government will reach, in its regular operations, the perfect balance between liberty and power.

The natural
cure for an ill-
administration,
in a popular or
representative
constitution,
is a change of men.

The independence
of judges once
destroyed, the
Constitution
is gone; it is a
dead letter.

... for it is a truth,
which the experience
of all ages has
attested, that the
people are commonly
most in danger when
the means of insuring
their rights are in the
possession of those of
whom they entertain
the least suspicion.

For my part, I
sincerely esteem the
Constitution, a system
which without the
finger of God, never
could have been
suggested and agreed
upon by such a
diversity of
interests.

If the representatives
of the people betray
their constituents,
there is then no
recourse left but in
the exertion of that
original right of
self-defense which
is paramount to all
positive forms of
government.

As to Taxes, they are
evidently inseparable
from Government. It is
impossible without them
to pay the debts of the
nation, to protect it
from foreign danger, or
to secure individuals
from lawless violence
and rapine.

In all very numerous
assemblies, of whatever
character composed,
passion never fails to
wrest the sceptre from
reason. Had every
Athenian citizen
been a Socrates, every
Athenian assembly
would still have
been a mob.

The origin of all civil government, justly established, must be a voluntary compact, between the rulers and the ruled; and must be liable to such limitations, as are necessary for the security of the absolute rights of the latter; for what original title can any man or set of men have, to govern others, except their own consent? To usurp dominion over a people, in their own despite, or to grasp at a more extensive power than they are willing to entrust, is to violate that law of nature, which gives every man a right to his personal liberty; and can, therefore, confer no obligation to obedience.

Civil liberty is
only natural liberty,
modified and secured
by the sanctions of
civil society. It is
not a thing, in its own
nature, precarious and
dependent on human
will and caprice; but it
is conformable to the
constitution of man, as
well as necessary to the
well-being of society.

The republican principle
demands that the deliberate
sense of the community
should govern the conduct of
those to whom they entrust
the management of their
affairs; but it does not
require an unqualified
complaisance to every
sudden breeze of passion or
to every transient impulse
which the people may receive
from the arts of men, who
flatter their prejudices to
betray their interests.

Common interest may always be reckoned upon as the surest bond of sympathy.

Every individual of the community at large has an equal right to the protection of government.

It is the advertiser who provides the paper for the subscriber. It is not to be disputed, that the publisher of a newspaper in this country, without a very exhaustive advertising support, would receive less reward for his labor than the humblest mechanic.

Allow a government to decline paying its debts and you overthrow all public morality -- you unhinge all the principles that preserve the limits of free constitutions. Nothing can more affect national prosperity than a constant and systematic attention to extinguish the present debt and to avoid as much as possibly the incurring of any new debt.

It is a singular advantage of taxes on articles of consumption that they contain in their own nature a security against excess. They prescribe their own limit, which cannot be exceeded without defeating the end purposed - that is, an extension of the revenue.

Unless your
government is
respectable,
foreigners will
invade your rights;
and to maintain
tranquillity you
must be respectable;
even to observe
neutrality you must
have a strong
government.

Were it not that it
might require too
long a discussion, it
would not be difficult
to demonstrate that
a large and well-
organized republic
can scarcely lose its
liberty from any other
cause than that of
anarchy, to which a
contempt of the laws
is the high-road.

Ah, this is the constitution. Now, mark my words. So long as we are a young and virtuous people, this instrument will bind us together in mutual interests, mutual welfare, and mutual happiness. But when we become old and corrupt, it will bind no longer.

For in politics,
as in religion, it is
equally absurd to aim
at making proselytes
by fire and sword.
Heresies in either
can rarely be cured
by persecution.

Safety from external danger is
the most powerful director of
national conduct. Even the
ardent love of liberty will,
after a time, give way to
its dictates. The violent
destruction of life and property
incident to war, the continual
effort and alarm attendant on a
state of continual danger, will
compel nations the most attached
to liberty to resort for repose
and security to institutions
which have a tendency to destroy
their civil and political
rights. To be more safe, they at
length become willing to run
the risk of being less free.

To cherish and stimulate the activity of the human mind, by multiplying the objects of enterprise, is not among the least considerable of the expedients, by which the wealth of a nation may be promoted. Even things in themselves not positively advantageous, sometimes become so, by their tendency to provoke exertion. Every new scene, which is opened to the busy nature of man to rouse and exert itself, is the addition of a new energy to the general stock of effort.

It will be forgotten,
on the one hand, that
jealousy is the usual
concomitant of violent
love, and that the noble
enthusiasm of liberty is
too apt to be infected with
a spirit of narrow and
illiberal distrust. On the
other hand, it will be
equally forgotten, that
the vigour of government
is essential to the
security of liberty.

The safety of a republic
depends essentially on
the energy of a common
national sentiment; on a
uniformity of principles
and habits; on the
exemption of the citizens
from foreign bias and
prejudice; and on that
love of country which
will almost invariably
be found to be closely
connected with birth,
education and family.

It has been frequently
remarked, that it seems to
have been reserved to the
people of this country to
decide, by their conduct
and example, the important
question, whether societies
of men are really capable or
not, of establishing good
government from reflection
and choice, or whether they
are forever destined to
depend, for their political
constitutions, on accident
and force.

No man in his
senses can hesitate
in choosing to be
free, rather than a
slave.

The rights of
neutrality will
only be respected,
when they are
defended by an
adequate power.

The true principle of a republic is that the people should choose whom they please to govern them. Representation is imperfect, in proportion as the current of popular favor is checked. The great source of free government, popular election, should be perfectly pure, and the most unbounded liberty allowed.

I would die to
preserve the law upon
a solid foundation;
but take away
liberty, and the
foundation is
destroyed.

When the sword is
once drawn, the
passions of men
observe no bounds
of moderation.

A nation has a
right to manage its
own concerns as it
thinks fit.

If mankind were to
resolve to agree in
no institution of
government, until
every part of it had
been adjusted to the
most exact standard
of perfection,
society would soon
become a general
scene of anarchy, and
the world a desert.

A fondness for
power is implanted
in most men, and it
is natural to abuse
it when acquired.

The passions of a
revolution are apt
to hurry even good
men into excesses.

Let Americans disdain
to be the instruments of
European greatness! Let
the thirteen States, bound
together in a strict and
indissoluble Union,
concur in erecting one
great American system,
superior to the control of
all transatlantic force or
influence, and able to
dictate the terms of the
connection between the
old and the new world!

The honor of a
nation is its life.
Deliberately to
abandon it is to
commit an act of
political suicide.

Divide et impera
must be the motto of
every nation that
either hates or
fears us.

I never expect to
see a perfect work from
imperfect man. The result
of the deliberations of all
collective bodies must
necessarily be a compound,
as well of the errors and
prejudices, as of the good
sense and wisdom, of the
individuals of whom they
are composed.

We are attempting, by
this Constitution, to
abolish factions, and
to unite all parties
for the general
welfare.

In a government framed for
durable liberty, not less
regard must be paid to
giving the magistrate a
proper degree of
authority, to make and
execute the laws with
rigour, than to guarding
against encroachments
upon the rights of the
community. As too much
power leads to despotism,
too little leads to
anarchy, and both
eventually to the
ruin of the people.

A garden, you know, is
a very usual refuge of a
disappointed politician.
Accordingly, I have
purchased a few acres
about nine miles from
town, have built a house,
and am cultivating
a garden.

To judge from the
history of mankind,
we shall be compelled
to conclude, that the
fiery and destructive
passions of war,
reign in the human
breast, with much
more powerful sway,
than the mild
and beneficent
sentiments of peace.

If duties are too high, they
lessen the consumption; the
collection is eluded; and
the product to the treasury
is not so great as when they
are confined within proper
and moderate bounds. This
forms a complete barrier
against any material
oppression of the citizens
by taxes of this class,
and is itself a natural
limitation of the power
of imposing them.

The laws of Congress
are restricted to a
certain sphere, and
when they depart from
this sphere, they are
no longer supreme
or binding.

Nothing could be more
ill-judged than that
intolerant spirit
which has, at all
times, characterized
political parties.

Foreign influence
is truly the Grecian
horse to a republic.
We cannot be too
careful to exclude
its influence.

It has been observed that a
pure democracy if it were
practicable would be the
most perfect government.
Experience has proved
that no position is
more false than this.
The ancient democracies
in which the people
themselves deliberated
never possessed one good
feature of government.
Their very character was
tyranny; their figure
deformity.

A share in the sovereignty of the state, which is exercised by the citizens at large, in voting at elections is one of the most important rights of the subject, and in a republic ought to stand foremost in the estimation of the law...That portion of the sovereignty, to which each individual is entitled, can never be too highly prized. It is that for which we have fought and bled.

Happy will it be for
ourselves, and most
honorable for human
nature, if we have
wisdom and virtue
enough to set so
glorious an example
to mankind!

It is far more
rational to suppose
that the courts were
designed to be an
intermediate body
between the people
and the legislature,
in order, among other
things, to keep the
latter within the
limits assigned to
their authority.

Give all power to the
many, they will oppress
the few. Give all power
to the few, they will
oppress the many. Both,
therefore, ought to
have the power, that
each may defend itself
against the other.

It is the Press which
has corrupted our
political morals -
and it is to the Press
we must look for the
means of our political
regeneration.

The representatives
of the people, in a popular
assembly, seem sometimes to
fancy that they are the
people themselves, and
betray strong symptoms of
impatience and disgust at
the least sign of opposition
from any other quarter; as if
the exercise of its rights,
by either the executive or
judiciary, were a breach of
their privilege and an
outrage to their dignity.

There is a certain
enthusiasm in liberty,
that makes human
nature rise above
itself, in acts of
bravery and heroism.

There are seasons in every country when noise and impudence pass current for worth; and in popular commotions especially, the clamors of interested and factious men are often mistaken for patriotism.

Energy in the executive
is a leading character in the
definition of good government.
It is essential to the
protection of the community
against foreign attacks; it is
not less essential to the steady
administration of the laws; to
the protection of property
against those irregular and
high-handed combinations
which sometimes interrupt the
ordinary course of justice; to
the security of liberty against
the enterprises and assaults of
ambition, of faction,
and of anarchy.

Experience teaches,
that men are often so
much governed by what
they are accustomed to
see and practice, that
the simplest and most
obvious improvements .
. . are adopted with
hesitation, reluctance,
and slow gradations.

Were not the disadvantages
of slavery too obvious to
stand in need of it, I might
enumerate and describe the
tedious train of calamities
inseparable from it. I might
show that it is fatal to
religion and morality; that
it tends to debase the mind,
and corrupt its noblest
springs of action. I might
show that it relaxes the
sinews of industry, clips
the wings of commerce, and
introduces misery and
indigence in every shape.

To watch the progress
of such endeavors is the
office of a free press.
To give us early alarm
and put us on our guard
against encroachments of
power. This then is a right
of utmost importance, one
for which, instead of
yielding it up, we ought
rather to spill our blood.

The law... dictated by
God Himself is, of
course, superior in
obligation to any
other. It is binding
over all the globe, in
all countries, and at
all times. No human
laws are of any
validity if
contrary
to this.

They are not rules prescribed by the sovereign to the subject, but agreements between sovereign and sovereign.

(On the New Constitution, The Federalist: (ed. 1810))

It will be of little avail
to the people, that the
laws are made by men of
their own choice, if the
laws be so voluminous
that they cannot be read,
or so incoherent that they
cannot be understood;
if they be repealed or
revised before they are
promulgated, or undergo
such incessant changes
that no man, who knows
what the law is to-day,
can guess what it will be
tomorrow.

Real firmness is
good for anything;
strut is good for
nothing.

The powers
contained in a
constitution...
ought to be
construed liberally
in advancement of
the public good.

It is a maxim deeply
ingrafted in that
dark system, that no
character, however
upright, is a match
for constantly
reiterated attacks,
however false.

Has it not...
invariably been
found that momentary
passions, and immediate
interests, have a more
active and imperious
control over human
conduct than general or
remote considerations
of policy, utility and
justice?

Americans rouse -
be unanimous, be
virtuous, be firm,
exert your courage,
trust in Heaven,
and nobly defy the
enemies both of God
and man!

The inquiry constantly
is what will please,
not what will benefit
the people. In such a
government there
can be nothing but
temporary expedient,
fickleness, and folly.

That experience is the
parent of wisdom is an
adage the truth of
which is recognized
by the wisest as well
as the simplest of
mankind.

In disquisitions of
every kind there are
certain primary
truths, or first
principles, upon
which all subsequent
reasoning must depend.

Remember civil and
religious liberty
always go together:
if the foundation of
the one be sapped, the
other will fall
of course.

A struggle for liberty
is in itself respectable
and glorious. . . .
When conducted with
magnanimity, justice and
humanity, it ought to
command the admiration
of every friend to human
nature. But if sullied
by crimes and
extravagances, it loses
its respectability.

The Liberty of the press
consists in the right to
publish with impunity
truth with good motives
for justifiable ends,
though reflecting on
government, magistracy,
or individuals.

The only distinction
between freedom and
slavery consists in this:
In the former state a man
is governed by the laws to
which he has given his
consent, either in person
or by his representative;
in the latter, he is
governed by the will of
another. In the one case,
his life and property are
his own; in the other, they
depend upon the pleasure
of his master. It is easy to
discern which of these two
states is preferable.

If it be asked, What is the most sacred duty and the greatest source of our security in a Republic? The answer would be, An inviolable respect for the Constitution and Laws — the first growing out of the last... A sacred respect for the constitutional law is the vital principle, the sustaining energy of a free government.

No person that has
enjoyed the sweets
of liberty can be
insensible of its
infinite value, or can
reflect on its reverse
without horror and
detestation.

Of those men who have
overturned the liberties
of republics, the
greatest number have
begun their career by
paying an obsequious
court to the people,
commencing demagogues
and ending tyrants.

A national debt if it is
not excessive will be to
us a national blessing;
it will be powerful
cement of our union.
It will also create a
necessity for keeping
up taxation to a degree
which without being
oppressive, will be a
spur to industry.

Men give me credit for
some genius. All the
genius I have lies in
this; when I have a
subject in hand, I study
it profoundly. Day and
night it is before me.
My mind becomes
pervaded with it.
Then the effort that I
have made is what people
are pleased to call the
fruit of genius. It is
the fruit of labor
and thought.

The true principle of government is this - make the system compleat in its structure; give a perfect proportion and balance to its parts; and the powers you give it will never affect your security.

That Americans are
entitled to freedom is
incontestable on every
rational principle. All
men have one common
original: they participate
in one common nature, and
consequently have one
common right. No reason
can be assigned why one man
should exercise any power
or preeminence over his
fellow-creatures more than
another; unless they have
voluntarily vested him
with it.

There is something so far-
fetched and so extravagant
in the idea of danger to
liberty from the militia
that one is at a loss whether
to treat it with gravity or
with raillery; whether to
consider it as a mere trial
of skill, like the paradoxes
of rhetoricians; as a
disingenuous artifice to
instil prejudices at any
price; or as the serious.

A feeble executive
implies a feeble
execution of the
government. A feeble
execution is but
another phrase for a
bad execution; and
a government ill
executed, whatever
may be its theory,
must be, in practice,
a bad government.

The regular distribution
of power into distinct
departments; the introduction of
legislative balances and checks;
the institution of courts
composed of judges holding their
offices during good behavior; the
representation of the people in
the legislature by deputies of
their own election . . . They are
means, and powerful means, by
which the excellences of
republican government may be
retained and its imperfections
lessened or avoided.

The voice of the people
has been said to be
the voice of God; and,
however generally this
maxim has been quoted
and believed, it is not
true to fact. The people
are turbulent and
changing, they seldom
judge or determine
right.

If the federal government
should overpass the just
bounds of its authority
and make a tyrannical use
of its powers, the people,
whose creature it is, must
appeal to the standard
they have formed, and take
such measures to redress
the injury done to the
Constitution as the
exigency may suggest
and prudence justify.

A habit of labor in the
people is as essential
to the health and
rigor of their minds
and bodies as it is
conducive to the
welfare of the state.